Michael Winicott

LINKEDIN FOR BUSINESS:
Network to grow your business

How to use Linkedin for networking, leads
generation and business development.

© 2015 by Michael Winicott.
© 2015 by UNITEXTO

Published by UNITEXTO

UNITEXTO
Digital Publishing

LINKEDIN FOR BUSINESS

Table of Contents

INTRODUCTION

CHAPTER 1: ABOUT LINKEDIN
What is it?
Who is in?
Why he or she is in and what they are looking for

CHAPTER 2: WHERE LINKEDIN WILL HELP
Branding
Marketing
Sales
Hiring

CHAPTER 3: SETTING UP A COMPANY BUSINESS
PAGE
Why set up a company business page
The LinkedIn Profile
Other info to include

CHAPTER 4: MARKETING TIPS

CHAPTER 5: GET MORE OUT OF LINKEDIN
Lead Generation
Ways to create leads

CONCLUSION

LINKEDIN FOR BUSINESS

INTRODUCTION:

Facebook.Official count: one billion three hundred million users. Google+. Official count: one billion six hundred million users. Instagram. Official count: three hundred million users. Twitter counts six hundred and fifty million users. The numbers are staggering about the users of the social networks.

In business terms it's an unlimited open market full of potential business opportunities of all kinds and for all industries that must be taken advantage of.

Yet, none of the above major social networks can help a company grow and achieve its objectives as much as LinkedIn, even though its users are "only" two hundred million. Why? Because of the demographics of LinkedIn. Who is in, why is he or she in and what is he or she looking for.

To put it simply, Twitter and Instagram are not setup for business. They are just for uploading texts and photos. Facebook and Google+ offer great opportunities for those who want to focus on a business –to-customer model of operations. LinkedIn is by far the best on business-to-business operation models which is easily transferable to the business-to-customer models and thus to everyone that is out there looking for something to buy online. This is what it was designed for.

In the following chapters we will present the issues and discuss the possibilities that LinkedIn offers to professionals. During the entire process you need to remember one thing: Social media is the way customers and other professionals want to learn. The old way of TV, radio and published commercials does not work as effectively as it used to any more. They represent the past. Social media represent the present and the future.

To paraphrase Forbes, based on the above concept, it's time to challenge the past and reassess the present to understand the future of marketing and sales. All the prospects and potential customers look to social media to connect. So must the professionals if they want to keep up with progress and their competition.

CHAPTER 1: ABOUT LINKEDIN

Let's start with the basics. What is LinkedIn?

As of May 2003 when it was first launched it is the first and so far the only social media network that has been designed right from the start to be business oriented. The premise of the design is to create profiles and connect with the other users in the network in an online version of real-time and real-world business relationships.

While the members connected may all be professionals, each member has the ability to invite anyone he or she wants to become a connection regardless of whether they are site users or not. In this manner the business-to-business initial relationship converts to a business-to-customer one at any time and the network each member creates can become multilayered by means of not only sales and services rendered, but also job opportunities, hiring personnel and in general any operations that can make a company grow.

Who is in?

The real secret of LinkedIn is its demographics. The vast majority is business people either by being company employees, or company CEOs or freelancers. However, the most important issue here is that most of them are decision makers.

The process of creating a relationship between these people is much faster as there are no intermediaries or paperwork involved. If the company business profile is accurate, updated and most of all true, then the relationship is formed in a couple of clicks.

This of course does not negate the need for official contracts and other such legal paperwork if the relationship advances to a real sale and cooperation one, but it does speed up the entire process by weeks and this alone is crucial in the modern world where speed and efficiency is at the top of the list of success.

Why he or she is in and what are they looking for

Imagine that you have established a business in a small town and that you have exhausted the opportunities offered by the local market. At that point you need to either move to a new market with all the problems that such a decision would bring along, or create a profile in LinkedIn and connect to the people that need your services or your products in other markets.

Once this connection is made then it's a simple matter of organizing the proper logistics and the new market is available both to you and your connection. And this is the main reason behind LinkedIn and what professionals are looking for there. The possibility of expanding their scope of operations to new markets.

Chapter 2: Where LinkedIn will Help

We have already discussed the general concept. Now it's time to discuss the details of what LinkedIn can actually do to help you achieve your business goals.

Branding

Every company and every professional always wants to build what will provide the best chances of success. A good and strong brand name. It's what people trust to award their business to. The usual way of establishing this brand name is an entire handbook. For LinkedIn it's just three steps.

➢ **Show you are an expert.**
People do not look for ordinary professionals. They look for people with real expertise in their profession. They are fed up with frauds. When you are building your profile you need to make sure it reflects the level of your professionalism and the level of expertise and knowledge you have for your trade.

➢ **Connect to the correct people.**

By the term connect, we mean not just you looking for people to connect to. We also mean people that will try to connect to you. The correct people are those who can help you achieve your objectives. Fellow alumni, colleagues, people in the same groups, people in the same line of work, past associates and referrals are the most likely candidates.

> ➢ **Build trust with these people to create meaningful relationships.**
> Trust is built by maintaining your contacts, reminding them of your existence and posting issues to establish credibility on your expert status and attain a thought leader status. In LinkedIn however, trust is also built by paying attention to details and showing beyond any reasonable doubt that you are for real and that you mean business.

Marketing

No matter how good in your trade you are, you cannot do anything if people do not know you. This is what marketing is there for. In the real world many things are accomplished by the word that is spoken from mouth to mouth. In LinkedIn this word is spoken from many mouths and heard by many ears at the same moment.

Marketing is an entirely different ball of wax and we will discuss the intricacies and some tips involved in a dedicated chapter to come.

Sales

Let's face it. No one goes professional just for the thrill or for the satisfaction. There is this little nagging matter of revenues involved which actually provide one with his or her livelihood. And that comes from selling either one's products or one's services.

On that front, LinkedIn provides the connections for you to use. The same principle of finding the right people is applicable here. The other businesses connected tell you what they are looking for. If you are what they are looking for they will contact you. If you have built up a profile that sells then if you connect with them they will become interested.

Hiring

This actually works both ways. You can find people to hire, or if you offer something employers like, you can get hired yourself. If you are an employer then LinkedIn offers you a set of recruiting tools to use and hire the talent that suites your purposes.

If you offer yourself up for hire, then using the same tools will let the employers that are looking for you, actually find you. The best way you sell yourself, the greater the chances of getting hired. Sales is not only about products or services. It's also about selling yourself as a person. It may sound slave-like but it is actually not.

Slaves are forced to work. You are not. You offer yourself and your skill set to be hired so that you can get a higher remuneration. In the real world you can only do so much at a time. In LinkedIn, all the employers that require someone like you, will get to take a look at you at once. One of them will offer you the appropriate incentives and the appropriate benefits to start working for them.

So far we have been discussing about the theory connected to LinkedIn. In the next chapter it is time to discuss what you actually have to do to take advantage of that it offers you. Create your page.

CHAPTER 3: SETTING UP A COMPANY BUSINESS PAGE

Why set up a company business page

Let's get a little deeper into the psychology of what is involved with people connecting to you and you connecting to them. The obvious issues are just the tip of the iceberg.

The current internet marketing practices involve sending loads of PDFs. Some of them are nicely designed, some of them are choreographed to perfection by internet marketing specialists and not the company itself, not to mention that a number of them flat out lie.

Everything is about trust. The knowledge that in B2B you can solve problems and get things done. The knowledge in B2C that what you offer is worth its value and more. People that stay connected to you monitor what you do. The progress of your business is indicated in your business page. And this progress is what in the final analysis builds the so much wanted and needed trust and creates customers and business partners that remain loyal to you.

Furthermore, through these connections people are treated as people and not faceless inserts in a mailing list. You know who is behind each connection. And they know you as who you are and not as another one that sends out a couple of million e-mails in the hope of getting a couple of clients.

The LinkedIn Profile

Now we've reached the heart and soul of the entire process. Everything depends on how you complete your profile. Here are a few secrets:

➢ **Do not leave fields uncompleted.**
It shows that you are not a true professional and that you do not pay the proper attention to detail. This is very detrimental and could cost you dearly.

➢ **Make sure that the first impression is not boring.**
This is the greatest mistake of them all. Your profile must look like no one else's, it must not be standard and it must not be filled with the usual pieces of information. Starting with a riveting cover photo and a compelling summary that includes everything that is of importance and updated regularly. People that

see the same info for the third time will not be of any use to you. They will not revisit your page either.

➢ **Do not forget the About Us link.**
This is the most usual mistake made in LinkedIn. The About Us link is way down at the bottom of the page. It is the most common of misconceptions that no one will ever scroll all that far down.

Remember trust? People that want to see what you are really all about want to see the full description of your company there, including links to your company profile, company history, achievements, etc...

Other info to include

Apart from your profile, your company page must include some info that will prompt the connection request if not force it. Here is a list:

✓ **Products and services**
It is a business page. Businesses have to do with products and services. It goes beyond words that the most important pieces of information are the products you sell or the

services that you provide. Start with the best product first or the service that you are best at. Remember to be honest about it. Do not mention characteristics your product does not have and do not mention services that you actually cannot deliver.

✓ **People**
If you employ personnel, you immediately fall to a different category of professionals. Asking your employees that already have LinkedIn accounts to connect to yours and identify themselves as your employees means that your prospects can obtain the information they need by contacting them directly. It also provides a sense of ordered structure in your company and a sense that you are a good employer.

✓ **Company Updates**
Your page must look creative and useful. As always with the internet sites it is the content that counts. Publishing company updates keeps your connections informed and keeps their interest in you alive.

✓ **Featured Updates**
The tool of Featured Updates is one of the most useful in LinkedIn. When you want to promote

a special event or a sale, or draw attention to something specific it comes in handy. It also shows that you pay attention to your page and that you want to make your page work for you.

✓ **Targeted Updates**

You may want to show a few things only to certain people. You can achieve that by using the targeted updates feature. The people you target this way will appreciate the effort and the preference and will build the relationship with you faster and deeper.

✓ **Promotion**

Link your LinkedIn site to your actual website and the people there. That way you can have people connected to you both through your domain and your LinkedIn site and keep up with your company's developments at a glance.

Now that your business page is up and running and containing all the necessary information, it's time to discuss the holy grail of business. How people will find out about you, or the process otherwise known as marketing.

CHAPTER 4: MARKETING TIPS

You go into looking for marketing solutions when you have something to offer out of which you expect to derive an income to pay the bills and survive upon. Internet marketing is a multifaceted, multi-layered, multi-detailed process that actually requires a specialist to bring forth the required results.

LinkedIn has actually simplified this process for you and all you need to do is follow a few tips and you're all set. Let's begin:

✓ **Business is Business**
It is a frequent announcement from all social media administrators, the police and organizations specializing in social media security that you should only connect to people you know or recognize. Some marketers also maintain that this kind of linking keeps the game fair.

This is not how business is conducted and this is not a directive to follow. Business is business and every single member of LinkedIn should get to know you. Remember that LinkedIn is primarily business. Not socialization.

✓ **Site customization**

As aforementioned, your page must not be boring. And there is nothing more boring than just a link to a website. Use a "call to action" feature to compel the people that visit your LinkedIn page to visit your actual site.

✓ **Recommendations**

The principle here is simple. The more you give the more you receive. The more you recommend others the more trust is built on you and the deeper your relations become. Especially if your recommendations help others. Just remember that it is even more appreciated and of even greater value, if you do not request that they return the favour. They will do it anyway on their own.

✓ **Join Groups**

The LinkedIn Groups are arguably the most important issue and the one that you should focus the most. Actually this is a two pronged feature.

The first one refers to being part of groups. It doesn't matter if they are related to your business interests or not. You need to consider these groups as independent networks where you are able to spread your message easily. Such networks allow for closer connection with your key partners and reaching a different business relationship level.

The second part comes with creating a group of your own. If you remember what we discussed earlier in this book, it is very important that you are considered as a thought leader. Owning groups will do that for you and will upgrade the potential of your overall opportunities even further.

✓ **Search ranking optimization**
LinkedIn works much like Google. Under the premise that people are constantly looking for people, products and services, with the search parameters not always being name and surname, the same principles of search engine optimization apply here as well.

The first thing to pay attention to is the headline of your profile which is the first impression. Use keywords in the headline. The next issues are related to your business ventures.

Both your current and past work experiences are crucial in the ranking system of LinkedIn along with any references you may have included as a specialty. Especially this last keyword search may make the difference to people searching for your particular talents but do not want to connect to someone generic.

The final aspect for a successful piece of marketing has to do with the advanced applications that LinkedIn has rolled out. There is an application for everyone and everything that can help you get what you want regardless of the industry you're in.

Always remember to visit the apps section of your profile. Out of the list, some of them are useful right away and you can use them to suite your purposes. If you need something and a suitable app is not available yet, revisiting the page will let you know if and when such an app will become available so that you can use it.

Up to know we have covered just about everything that you need to know about how to make LinkedIn work for you. As said, just about. There still are some things you can do to squeeze every last ounce of benefits. Just keep reading the next chapter.

CHAPTER 5: GET MORE OUT OF LINKEDIN

So far we have explored the possibilities offered by LinkedIn in reference to business ventures, what to do to setup your business page and your profile and how to build the network that will get you closer to your goals.

Do all the above lead to revenues? Do all the above lead to sales and profits? The answer is yes if you manage to make your network generate leads that will lead to conversions.

The world of online business works as follows:

➢ **Leads**
Generating leads is to generate an interest to what you sell or what services you provide. By building your network of connections, entering into groups, creating groups of your own and in general following the marketing tips of chapter 4, you become visible. People can find you. That's step number one.

By completing your profile and customizing your business page to reflect your products and your services along with their level of quality, you provide your network with the means to become interested in what you have to offer.

And that's the definition of generating leads through LinkedIn.

> **Prospects**

However, that was only the beginning of the process. People became interested in what you offer. So what? Did you make the sale? Did you sign a contract for your services? Not yet.

When people become interested they want all the pertinent information. If they have it all right there either on your LinkedIn page or through the connections to your own sites, they become prospects for business. If the answers they find are satisfactory then they move to the next step which is

> **Conversions**

That's the term used online for people who reached your online gate of sales or service provision and converted their interest to an actual purchase or a hiring bringing you revenues in return. And that's the whole point of the exercise.

However, there is a little bit more involved into generating leads than just building up a network of connections. Here are a few more secrets of the trade:

➢ **Invest some time per day.**
   To actually do two things:

   The first one is to click on the "connect" button of the list that LinkedIn sends to your feed with "people you may know". As aforementioned, business is business. You are not looking for friends you are looking to expand your business options. Clicking on that button will expand your network and will bestow upon you the name of "network expander" which is a very important step into lead generation.

   The second is to study the connections of your connections. In the lists of the people directly linked to your network there may be people that you do not know but you may want to get to know. And by that we mean to get them interested enough to generate a lead that will convert.

➢ **Follow them to follow you.**
   Business works both ways. You need to make revenue from your connections. They need to make revenues as well. May be not from you but if you follow your partners and you

monitor their pages you may be able to help them gain some more revenues. And then you may expect a reciprocating gesture.

➢ **Know when to stop.**
LinkedIn IS NOT and SHOULD NOT IS a six to eight hours' worth of work per day for a week and then do nothing more for a month and then repeat the same process again.

After the initial stages it only takes 20 to 30 minutes per day to achieve your goals. A month later you will start receiving the first tangible results. Afterwards it's just a matter of keeping up the good work and always make sure that everything new gets posted.

The record shows that 84% of the companies and businesses that took advantage of what LinkedIn had to offer over the past two years saw a notable to significant increase in their sales, revenues and most of all their brand name which has become a trustworthy one with loyal followers. Is there any reason for you not to be included in this 84%?

CONCLUSION:

LinkedIn simply means business. It was designed for business, it is addressing business people and it aims to provide the business world with the means to do their jobs effectively and to expand their business opportunities and options as much as possible.

The administrators of LinkedIn saw fit to provide the network members with a multitude of tools and a multitude of options to do what it takes to achieve their goals. However, it is still up to each professional to make the appropriate decisions and choices.

Going pro means a few obligations. No matter what industry you are in. It means hard work to either produce goods that other people want or to become one of the best in your line of services so that people may choose you over your competition. But most of all, going pro means building trust.

Trust between you and your business partners. Trust between you and your customers. Trust between you and the people that may become interested in what you have to offer. To build that trust you need to do a few things if you choose to use LinkedIn much in the same way that you would have to, if you stayed with the traditional form of doing business.

Complete your profile so that people may know exactly who they are dealing with. Setup your page so that people may be able to find you. Build your networks, join and create groups and follow a few tested and successful marketing tips so that you become as visible as possible and build a good and strong brand name.

Help your partners when they need to. Follow and monitor them. They will do the same for you. Refer them to others and you will find yourself referred to others.

There is one axiom in business. Give to take. Use LinkedIn to give and LinkedIn will see to it that you will take.